from ...
by way ... *co*

2012

The Best 50
GARLIC
RECIPES

David DiResta

BRISTOL PUBLISHING ENTERPRISES
HAYWARD, C ALIFORNIA

Printed in the United States of America.

ISBN-13: 978-1-55867-345-8
ISBN-10: 1-55867-345-8
Cover design: Frank J. Paredes

GARLIC VARIETIES

The **white bulb** *(Allium sativum),* called American or California garlic, produces very intense cloves. The **purple and rose bulbs** *(Allium sativum)*, called Mexican or Italian garlic, also produce strong cloves. The large, white **elephant garlic bulb** *(Allium ampelo-prasum)* yields milder cloves. An elephant garlic bulb can grow up to the size of an orange, with cloves weighing 1 ounce each. **Green garlic** is young garlic before it begins to form cloves. It has a milder flavor. The tops can be thinly sliced and used as a garnish.

PURCHASING GARLIC

When purchasing fresh garlic, be sure it is solid and firm. Fresh garlic has superior flavor to dehydrated and processed forms, but the alternatives can be useful, and are better than nothing. $\frac{1}{8}$ teaspoon dehydrated powder, minced garlic or garlic flakes, is equal to 1 fresh clove. Garlic salt is about 90 percent salt and should be used in place of salt in a recipe. About $\frac{1}{2}$ teaspoon garlic salt will substitute for 1 fresh clove. Preminced or prechopped garlic preserved in liquid and sold at supermarkets in small jars is fairly close to fresh garlic and is a convenient time-saver.

HEALTH BENEFITS

Garlic has a very long reputation as a purifying herb, used as an internal as well as an external bacteria killer. Garlic reduces LDL-cholesterol ("bad") and increases HDL-cholesterol ("good"). Recently, it has been shown that allicin, the substance in garlic that gives it its strong flavor, is similar to a European drug used to expel mucus and has been shown to be effective against colds; if mothers eat garlic at least 1 hour before breast feeding, it can help stimulate the baby's appetite; sulfur compounds in garlic have anti-coagulant effects, preventing blood clots.

TIPS FOR PREPARING AND COOKING GARLIC

For the best flavor, cut garlic by hand with a knife: this releases only a small amount of the oil. Second choice, for convenience, is a garlic press. To remove the peel from a clove before chopping, place it on your cutting board and press down on it with the side of a knife: this will make the peel come off easily.

BEWARE THE HAZARDS OF IMPROPER STORAGE

If stored properly, garlic should remain fresh for up to one month. Keep garlic in a cool, dry place, but not in the refrigerator. A well-vented ceramic pot creates the ideal environment to ensure freshness. Don't separate the cloves from the bulb or peel the garlic until you are ready to use it in the recipe. If a garlic bulb should start to sprout, it's still fine to consume. However, the flavor will not be as intense, so the quantity may have to be increased.

Garlic braids have offered a convenient and decorative method of storing garlic bulbs (and in some cultures, keeping evil spirits at bay) for centuries. Braid garlic by the stalks, removing bulbs one at a time, as needed.

The Food and Drug Administration (FDA) has issued a warning to consumers that homemade mixes of garlic in oil, garlic in butter and garlic in margarine should be kept refrigerated. The FDA recommends that consumers use infused oil mixtures shortly after making them and that they refrigerate all oil mixtures and discard them immediately if they are suspected of being spoiled.

I recommend that you refrigerate infused oil mixtures such as *Red Raspberry and Garlic Vinaigrette*, page 19, *Garlicky Vinaigrette*, page 22, *Tomato Garlic Vinaigrette*, page 23, and all other recipes that contain oil and garlic for *only two days*.

THE COOK'S TOOLS

You can purchase these tools through www.artisancookshop.com.

garlic press: a kitchen tool used to press a garlic clove through small holes, extracting pulp and juice. A top-quality garlic press is indispensable. Purchase a sturdy metal press with a high extrusion rate.

garlic cellar/keeper: a covered container made of stoneware, terra cotta or porcelain provides the ideal environment for storing garlic.

garlic peeler: Place 1 garlic clove in the peeler basket. Press the handle tightly, and a peeled clove of garlic falls through the bottom. It's ideal for peeling large quantities of garlic in a short period.

odor remover: a small, 3-x-2-inch flat bar made from a metal alloy that completely washes away the garlic odor. Simply rub the bar over your hands under cool running water. The bar causes a reaction that releases the garlic oils from your skin. For best results, wash your hands as soon as possible.

garlic baker: a unique, easy-to-use kitchen accessory designed specifically for baking garlic. Baked garlic has less pungency and a much sweeter, subtler flavor. Season the garlic before baking and add it to seafood, poultry, meats and pasta dishes, or simply spread it on crackers or hot crusty breads. Garlic bakers are available in several styles and can accommodate from 1 to 5 bulbs.

garlic slicer/shredder: a handy, innovative kitchen accessory that is ideal for cutting large quantities of garlic in uniform slices. It resembles a mandolin but is much smaller in size. Made with strong, sharp stainless steel blades, it has a well-designed holder for securing garlic cloves while protecting your fingers. The reversible blade is excellent for preparing fine shredded garlic.

BRUSCHETTA

This appetizer is good to eat hot or cold. Be sure to use extra virgin olive oil and fresh tomatoes for a spirited flavor. Substitute mozzarella cheese for the fontina.

6 slices wide country or Italian bread, 1 inch thick
1/3 cup extra virgin olive oil
4 cloves garlic, minced or pressed

2 cups diced tomatoes
6 marinated artichoke hearts
1 cup grated fontina cheese
1/2 tsp. dried basil

Heat oven to 400°. Toast or grill both sides of bread. Combine olive oil and garlic in a small skillet and sauté over medium heat for 2 minutes. Generously brush one side of each slice of bread with garlic oil. Cover oiled bread with a layer of tomatoes. Top with artichoke hearts and cheese. Sprinkle with basil. Place on a baking sheet and bake for 10 minutes. Heat under the broiler for 2 minutes.

GARLIC CHEESE SPREAD

Serve chilled as a dip or spread with fresh vegetables or crackers.

1 bulb *Roasted Garlic,* page 26
4 oz. Gorgonzola cheese, cut into 1-inch pieces
8 oz. cream cheese, softened
1½ tsp. dried parsley
1½ tsp. dried basil

Squeeze soft garlic from roasted cloves. Combine garlic and remaining ingredients with a food processor or blender and process into a creamy spread. Transfer to a serving bowl and refrigerate for at least 2 hours, until ready to serve.

GARLIC SALSA

Serve with Garlic Pita Chips, *page 10, or as a topping for baked poultry or fish.*

6 cloves garlic, minced or pressed
1 can (1 lb. 12 oz.) crushed tomatoes in puree
1/4 cup chopped fresh cilantro
1/4 cup chopped scallions
1 tsp. fresh lime juice
2 tbs. chopped jalapeño peppers
1 tbs. chili powder

In a large bowl, combine all ingredients and mix well. Refrigerate for at least 2 hours.

GARLIC HUMMUS

This version of the traditional Middle Eastern appetizer has a little zing. Try using a wooden lemon reamer to easily remove the juice and pulp from the lemons. Serve as a delicious dip with fresh pita bread slices or sliced carrots and other raw vegetables.

1 can (15 oz.) garbanzo beans, rinsed and drained
1/4 cup tahini (sesame seed paste)
2 tbs. water
1 tbs. olive oil
juice and pulp of 2 lemons, seeds removed
6 cloves garlic, pressed
1 tsp. chili powder
1/4 tsp. freshly ground pepper
1/8 tsp. salt
1/4 tsp. paprika

Combine all ingredients, except paprika, with a food processor. Process for 4 minutes, or until smooth. Scoop into a serving bowl and sprinkle with paprika. Refrigerate for 2 hours. Serve chilled.

GARLIC PITA CHIPS

Servings: 6

Delicious and addictive. I enjoy these served with cold Garlic Salsa, *page 8. They can be prepared a day in advance.*

2 tbs. butter	8 cloves garlic, pressed
½ cup olive oil	6 loaves pita bread

Heat oven to 350°. Melt butter in a small saucepan. Add olive oil and garlic to melted butter and sauté over low heat for 10 minutes. Split open pita pockets and cut in half. Each pita will make 4 half-moon shapes. With rough side up, lay pita slices on a baking sheet. Brush entire surface with garlic mixture. Bake for 10 minutes. Place under the broiler for 1 minute, or until golden brown. Remove from oven and place on paper towels to absorb excess oil. Break into 2-inch pieces and serve in a large bowl or towel-lined wicker basket. For a variation, sprinkle with dried basil or oregano before baking.

GARLIC BREAD

Garlic bread was probably invented in the United States during the era of Italian-American restaurants in the late 1940s. You can also use Italian bread.

1 loaf French bread, halved lengthwise
4 cloves garlic, cut in half
$\frac{1}{2}$ cup butter

Place bread under the broiler and toast lightly, carefully watching to avoid burning. Remove bread from oven and quickly rub crusty surface with cut garlic. Butter bread. Serve immediately, or reheat in the oven for 3 to 5 minutes before serving.

GARLIC HERB BUTTER

Makes 1/2 cup

Use for warm bread or rolls, or when cooking fish, lamb, vegetables or poultry. For an elegant touch, place the butter in the freezer for 20 minutes, and use a butter curler to scrape sculptured swirls.

1/2 cup butter or margarine, softened
2 cloves garlic, pressed
1/2 tsp. dried basil
1/2 tsp. dried thyme

Combine all ingredients in a food processor workbowl or blend together in a small bowl with a fork or spoon. Keep refrigerated or freeze for future use.

RIO RANCHERO SEAFOOD SALSA

Servings: 4-6

Serve with Garlic Pita Chips, page 10, as a topping for tacos or as a meal in itself — the fresh garlic and seafood come together beautifully for a spicy and nutritious meal.

1 can (28 oz.) crushed tomato in puree
1 medium onion, finely chopped
6 cloves garlic, minced or pressed
2 tbs. chopped jalapeño peppers
1 tbs. chili powder
1 can (4.5 oz.) mild green chile peppers
1 tsp. chopped fresh cilantro
1/2 lb. cooked small shrimp, or large shrimp cut into bite-sized pieces
1/2 lb. cooked crabmeat, cut into bite-sized pieces

In a large bowl, combine crushed tomato, onion, garlic, peppers, chili powder, chile peppers and cilantro. Mix thoroughly. Stir in shrimp and crabmeat. Cover bowl and refrigerate for at least 2 hours. Serve chilled.

GARLIC AND HERB FOCACCIA

Servings: 8-12

This flavorful focaccia goes well with just about any dish. Use a food processor, heavy-duty mixer or bread machine, if desired.

1 pkg. active dry yeast
1 cup plus 1 tbs. warm water
1 tbs. sugar
3 1/4 cups all-purpose flour
1/2 tsp. salt

5 tbs. olive oil
2 cloves garlic, pressed
1/2 tsp. ground dried rosemary
1/2 tsp. dried basil

In a small bowl, dissolve yeast in water and add sugar. Set aside for 5 minutes. In a large bowl, combine flour and salt. Mix well. Add yeast mixture, 3 tbs. of the olive oil and garlic and stir together to form a ball. Place dough on a floured surface and knead for 10 minutes. Place dough in a greased bowl, cover with plastic wrap and let rise for 1 1/2 hours in a draft-free area.

Heat oven to 400°. Punch down dough and let rest for 10 minutes. Roll out dough to fit an 8½-x-12-inch baking pan. Brush bottom and sides of pan with olive oil. Place dough in pan, pressing and stretching so it extends to all sides of pan. Pierce dough with a fork about every 2 to 3 inches and brush top with olive oil. Sprinkle with rosemary and basil. Bake for 25 minutes. Brush top with remaining olive oil and broil for 3 to 5 minutes, or until top is golden brown. Serve hot or at room temperature.

GARLIC ONION SOUP

Serve as a first course or as an accompaniment to a fresh salad or sandwich.

1 bulb *Roasted Garlic,* page 26
3 tbs. butter
5 medium onions, thinly sliced
1 can (13¾ oz.) beef broth

7 cups water
4 beef bouillon cubes
1 tbs. Worcestershire sauce
Garlic Croutons, page 38

Squeeze roasted garlic from each clove and set aside. Melt butter in a skillet. Add onion slices and sauté over medium-low heat, uncovered, for 30 minutes. In a large saucepan, combine beef broth, water, bouillon cubes, Worcestershire sauce and roasted garlic. Simmer for 30 minutes. Remove broth mixture from heat and cool; pour into a food processor or blender and puree. You may have to process this in two or three batches. Return pureed mixture to stockpot. Add sautéed onions and simmer for 30 minutes. Serve in individual soup bowls with *Garlic Croutons*.

GARLIC CROUTONS

Serve with soups or salads for a spicy treat. This is a clever way to use stale bread.

3 cups (about 6 slices) day-old Italian bread, crusts removed, cut
  into ³/₄-inch cubes
¹/₄ cup unsalted butter
3 cloves garlic, minced or pressed
¹/₂ tsp. dried basil
¹/₂ tsp. dried parsley

Prepare bread cubes and set aside. Melt butter in a nonstick skillet over medium heat. Add garlic, basil and parsley. Add bread, reduce heat to medium-low and sauté for 4 to 5 minutes. Stir constantly. Remove from heat and place croutons on baking sheets. Bake in a 325° oven for 25 minutes, or until golden brown. Stir occasionally.

SAUSAGE SOUP WITH SPINACH AND RICE

Servings: 6

This soup has a spicy kick. Serve it with a salad and crusty bread.

1 lb. hot Italian sausage
1 tbs. olive oil
1 cup chopped onion
3 cloves garlic, crushed
9 cups chicken broth
1/2 cup diced tomatoes, with juice
3 tbs. tomato paste

1 tsp. dried oregano
1 tsp. dried basil
3 cups fresh baby spinach, torn
    into 2–3 inch pieces
2 cups cooked long-grain rice
salt and pepper to taste
1/4 cup grated Parmesan cheese

Sauté sausage in a large stockpot over medium-high heat until cooked, about 10 minutes. Remove from pot and discard drippings. Add olive oil to pot and heat. Add onion and sauté for 3 to 4 minutes, until translucent. Add garlic and sauté for 1 minute. Return sausage to pot. Add broth, tomatoes, tomato paste, oregano and basil. Simmer for 20 minutes. Add spinach and rice and simmer until spinach is just wilted. Serve topped with Parmesan cheese.

TABOULLEH

Parsley and lemon bring out the flavors of the vegetables and spices in this Middle Eastern salad . Arrange some taboulleh on a large platter with leafy greens, hummus, olives and grilled pita wedges for a Mediterranean "antipasto." Or just serve with pita bread.

$\frac{1}{2}$ cup bulghur wheat
1 cup water
2 cups chopped fresh parsley,
   firmly packed
1 small cucumber, finely chopped
1 large tomato, finely chopped
3 red onions, finely chopped

2 tbs. finely chopped fresh mint
$\frac{1}{4}$ tsp. freshly ground pepper
2 cloves garlic, minced or pressed
$\frac{1}{4}$ cup (about 1$\frac{1}{2}$ lemons) fresh
   lemon juice
1 tbs. olive or canola oil

Combine bulghur wheat and water and soak for 2 hours. In a large bowl, combine parsley, cucumber, tomato, onions, mint and pepper. Mix thoroughly. Drain bulghur and combine with vegetables and spices. Add garlic and lemon juice. Slowly stir in oil. Mix and refrigerate for at least 3 hours before serving.

RED RASPBERRY VINEGAR

Makes about 2½ cups

¼ cup blueberries, fresh or frozen
½ cup red raspberries, fresh or frozen
½ cup cranberries, fresh or frozen
2 cups white wine vinegar
¼ cup clover honey
2 cinnamon sticks
2 whole cloves

Thaw berries if frozen. Bring vinegar to a low boil in a saucepan. Reduce heat to simmer. Add honey, blueberries, ¼ cup raspberries and ¼ cup cranberries. Cool for 1 hour. Strain through a very fine mesh stainless steel strainer or cheesecloth. Pour vinegar into sterilized wine bottles or glass jars. Add remaining berries and spices. Seal containers with tight-fitting corks and store in a dark, dry area for 2 weeks.

RED RASPBERRY AND GARLIC VINAIGRETTE

Makes ½ cup

Use this special dressing for salads or as a marinade for poultry and seafood.

6 tbs. Red Raspberry Vinegar
2 tbs. olive oil
2 cloves garlic, pressed

2 tsp. minced fresh basil
1 tsp. Dijon mustard

Vigorously mix all ingredients in a bowl or bottle. Refrigerate. Shake well to use.

GARLIC VINEGAR

Makes 1½ cups

For subtle garlic flavor, use this when regular vinegar is called for.

12 oz. wine vinegar
5 cloves garlic, minced or pressed

Combine garlic and vinegar in a clear glass bottle. Carefully seal bottle and store for 2 weeks in a well-lighted area. Strain garlic from vinegar. Store in a cool, dark area.

GARLICKY VINAIGRETTE

Pour over or toss with a fresh garden salad or cold pasta salad. Also works great as a marinade for meats, poultry, fish or vegetables. Make a fresh batch of vinaigrette each time. Refrigerate; do not store for longer than a day or two.

3 tbs. balsamic vinegar
3/4 cup extra virgin olive oil
1/4 tsp. freshly ground pepper
2 cloves garlic, minced or pressed
2 tsp. chopped fresh basil
1 tbs. fresh lemon juice

In a medium bowl, combine all ingredients and whisk until well blended.

TOMATO GARLIC VINAIGRETTE

Servings: 6-8

This is delicious over leafy greens, tomatoes and cucumbers. Mustard lovers can add 1 tbs. Dijon mustard to ingredients for extra flavor.

1 cup tomato juice
2 cloves garlic, minced or pressed
1/4 cup extra virgin olive oil
1/8 tsp. dried basil
1/8 tsp. dried parsley
1/8 tsp. freshly ground pepper
3 tbs. balsamic vinegar

In a medium bowl, combine all ingredients and whisk until well blended. Refrigerate.

BASIC GARLIC DRESSING AND MARINADE

Makes 1/3 cup

Serve on antipasto or a garden salad, or as a marinade for meats.

¼ cup extra virgin olive oil
2 tbs. white or red wine vinegar
2 cloves garlic, minced or pressed

¼ tsp. freshly ground pepper
salt to taste

Combine all ingredients in a small bowl and mix thoroughly.

GARLIC-LEMON PEPPERCORNS

Makes about ¼ cup

Invest in a high-quality pepper mill. Freshly ground pepper will enhance your foods. This flavored pepper adds zest to any dish.

3 tbs. cracked black
  peppercorns

2¼ tsp. dried minced garlic
1 tsp. dried lemon peel

Mix all ingredients together and grind in a pepper mill or with a mortar and pestle.

GARLIC AND HONEY DRESSING

Enhance the flavor of a well-made salad with this interesting dressing.

2 tbs. white or red wine vinegar
¼ tsp. sea salt
¼ tsp. freshly ground pepper
1 clove garlic, minced or pressed
½ tsp. Dijon mustard
1 tsp. honey
⅓ cup extra virgin olive oil
1 tbs. chopped fresh basil

Combine vinegar, salt, pepper, garlic, mustard and honey in a small bowl. Mix thoroughly. Slowly add olive oil, stirring constantly. Add basil and blend. Store in an airtight container. Shake before using.

ROASTED GARLIC

Roasted garlic is not strong-tasting: it has a delicious sweet fla-vor. Serve roasted garlic warm as a spread, or use in other recipes. Increase recipe size as needed.

1 large bulb garlic
1/4 tsp. or 1 tbs. olive oil (see
    method)
1 tsp. butter, optional

1/8 tsp. dried basil
1/8 tsp. dried thyme
freshly ground pepper to taste

Heat oven to 350°. For perfectly roasted garlic, cut 1/4 inch from top of garlic bulb. Remove loose outer leaves. Bulb should remain intact. Pour 1/4 tsp. olive oil over bulb and dot with butter, or pour 1 tbs. olive oil over bulb and eliminate butter. Sprinkle with basil, thyme and pepper. Place cover on garlic baker. For a medium to large bulb, bake for 50 minutes. For an extra large bulb, bake for an additional 10 minutes. If cooking in a microwave oven, prepare bulb as directed and cook on high for 1 1/2 minutes. Separate cloves and squeeze out garlic.

MARINARA SAUCE

Servings: 4

This appetizing sauce is delicious with pasta and other cooked foods.

2 tbs. olive oil
3 cloves garlic, minced or pressed
1 medium onion, finely chopped
2 cans (28 oz. each) Italian plum tomatoes, chopped and mashed
$\frac{1}{2}$ tsp. dried oregano
2 tbs. chopped fresh basil
$\frac{1}{4}$ tsp. freshly ground pepper
$\frac{1}{8}$ tsp. salt

Heat olive oil in a medium saucepan over medium heat. Add garlic and onion and sauté for 5 to 7 minutes, or until onions are soft. Add tomatoes. Stir in oregano, basil, pepper and salt. Partially cover saucepan. Reduce heat and simmer for $1\frac{1}{2}$ hours. Stir occasionally.

ROASTED GARLIC AND SPINACH QUICHE

Serve this crustless quiche as a side dish or for luncheon as the main attraction. To assure a perfect texture, carefully drain cooked spinach of all water.

1 bulb *Roasted Garlic,* page 26
1 tbs. butter
1 small onion, finely chopped
4 eggs
1 cup milk
$1/4$ tsp. chili powder
$1/2$ tsp. salt
$1/4$ tsp. freshly ground pepper
1 cup cooked spinach, fresh or frozen, drained well
$1/2$ cup shredded Monterey Jack cheese
$1/4$ tsp. vegetable oil for oiling pan

Heat oven to 350°. Separate roasted garlic cloves, peel and mash in a small bowl to form a paste. Melt butter in a skillet. Add onion and sauté until soft, about 6 minutes. Add garlic paste and sauté for 4 minutes. Blend together and set aside. In a medium bowl, whisk together eggs, milk, chili powder, salt and pepper. In another bowl, combine garlic-onion mixture with spinach and cheese. Mix well. Spread spinach mixture firmly in a lightly oiled 9-inch quiche or pie pan. Pour egg mixture evenly over spinach.

Bake for 40 minutes. Quiche is done when a toothpick inserted in the center comes out clean.

ROASTED GARLIC BREAD

Servings: 8

Roasted garlic and fresh-baked bread are just meant for each other.

2 bulbs *Roasted Garlic,* page 26
1 tbs. olive oil
2 tbs. grated Parmesan cheese
½ tsp. dried basil

¼ tsp. dried oregano
¼ tsp. dried parsley
¼ tsp. freshly ground pepper
1 loaf crusty bread or baguette

Heat oven to 350°. Separate roasted garlic cloves, peel and mash in a small bowl to form a paste. Combine garlic paste with all remaining ingredients, except bread. Mix thoroughly. Slice bread in half lengthwise, separating top from bottom. Spread garlic mixture on inside of each half. Wrap each half in parchment paper or foil and bake for 10 minutes. Remove parchment paper or foil wrap from bread and place under the broiler for 2 to 3 minutes.

Or if you prefer, cut bread in slices and spread garlic mixture between bread slices. Wrap bread with foil and bake in a 350° oven for 20 minutes. Serve warm.

FRESH SPINACH WITH GARLIC

Spinach is great with garlic. But spinach does not store very well. Buy it fresh and cook it within two days. This is a perfect accompaniment for a seafood dish.

3/4 lb. fresh spinach
1/3 cup olive oil
4 cloves garlic, thinly sliced

1/2 tsp. dried basil
1/2 tsp. freshly ground pepper

Wash spinach thoroughly under cold running water. Be sure to remove all the grit. Cut out tough stems and leave spinach whole or break into large pieces. Place spinach in a medium saucepan in 1 inch water. Pour olive oil over spinach. Mix in garlic slices and sprinkle with basil and pepper. Bring to a boil.

Cover, reduce heat to medium and cook for 5 to 7 minutes, or until tender. Serve in individual serving bowls with garlic-flavored liquid.

SAUTÉED BRUSSELS SPROUTS WITH GARLIC

Servings: 4

Bright green Brussels sprouts complement the mushrooms and pepper beautifully for an eye-appealing and tasty dish.

1 lb. fresh Brussels sprouts
2 tbs. vegetable or canola oil
3 cloves garlic, minced or pressed
1 cup thinly sliced mushrooms
1 red bell pepper, cut into matchstick strips
2 tbs. *Garlic Herb Butter*, page 23
1/4 cup roasted pecans or cashews, optional

Remove outer leaves and cut Brussels sprouts into quarters. Heat oil in a large skillet. Add garlic and sauté for 1 minute. Add Brussels sprouts, mushrooms and pepper. Sauté for 5 to 7 minutes. Transfer to a serving bowl and toss with *Garlic Herb Butter*. For added flavor and crunch, sprinkle with roasted pecans or cashews after cooking.

STRING BEAN AND GARLIC MIX

Servings: 4

This deeply flavorful vegetable dish tastes great hot or cold. It's a good addition to a picnic, and it's easy to prepare, too.

1 lb. string beans
3 tbs. olive oil
3/4 tsp. garlic powder

1/4 tsp. dried basil
freshly ground pepper to taste

Snip tips off both ends of beans with kitchen shears or cut off with a sharp knife. Break beans in half and wash under cold running water. Place beans in a 2 1/2- to 3 1/2-quart saucepan with 1 inch water and steam or boil until tender, about 4 minutes.

Remove beans, without liquid, from saucepan. If you are serving them cold, plunge beans into cold water for 1 to 2 minutes, drain and place in a storage container or bowl. If you are serving them hot, remove to a serving bowl. Add olive oil, garlic powder, basil and pepper. Mix thoroughly. Serve hot or refrigerate and serve cold.

GARLICKY VEGETABLE SAUTÉ

Servings: 2

This spicy and satisfying vegetable recipe can easily be increased if you need more servings.

2 tbs. olive or vegetable oil
½ tsp. paprika
½ cup sliced scallions
4 cloves garlic, minced or
  pressed
1 medium red bell pepper, cut
  into thin matchstick strips
1 medium green bell pepper,
  cut into thin matchstick strips
1 medium yellow summer
  squash, sliced into ⅛-inch
  rounds
1 medium zucchini, sliced into
  ⅛-inch rounds
¼ tsp. freshly ground pepper

Heat oil in a large skillet over medium heat. Add paprika and stir thoroughly. Add scallions and garlic; sauté for 2 minutes. Add all other ingredients, partially cover and sauté over medium-low heat for 15 to 17 minutes, or until vegetables are tender, stirring occasionally.

GARLIC AND HONEY CARROTS

Choose young, tender carrots for a sweet, full flavor. You'll cook this dish again!

3 cups carrots, cut into ¼-inch rounds
2 tbs. butter
1 tbs. honey
1 clove garlic, minced or pressed
1 tsp. minced onion
2 tbs. raisins
1 tsp. brown sugar, packed
¼ tsp. dried dill weed

Place carrots in a vegetable steamer with 1 inch water. Bring to a boil and steam for 5 to 7 minutes, or until carrots are tender-crisp.

Make sauce: While carrots are cooking, combine, butter, honey, garlic, onion, raisins, brown sugar and dill weed in a small saucepan. Cook over low heat until onion and garlic are soft.

Combine carrots and sauce in a serving bowl. Mix thoroughly. Serve warm.

HEAVENLY RICE AND SPINACH

Servings: 4–6

Leave standard potatoes or plain cooked rice behind!

1/8 cup toasted pine nuts
1 1/2 cups long-grain white rice
5 tbs. butter
6 cloves garlic, minced or pressed
2 medium onions, finely chopped
1/4 tsp. salt
1/4 tsp. freshly ground pepper
4 cups chopped fresh spinach, packed
3/4 cup chicken stock
1/2 cup freshly grated Parmesan cheese

Roast pine nuts in a dry skillet over medium heat, stirring constantly until golden brown. Set aside. Prepare rice according to package instructions. Melt butter in a large skillet. Add garlic and onions and sauté for 5 minutes. Add salt, pepper and spinach and sauté for 3 minutes, or until spinach becomes limp.

Add chicken stock and cooked rice. Sauté for 5 minutes, or until rice is steaming hot. Stir in Parmesan cheese and toasted pine nuts. Remove from heat. Keep covered and serve warm.

STUFFED BAKED POTATOES

Roasted garlic stuffing blends very nicely with Parmesan cheese.

8 cloves *Roasted Garlic,* page 26
4 large baking potatoes
2 tsp. minced fresh or freeze-
dried chives
½ cup milk
¼ cup butter, melted
3 tbs. grated Parmesan cheese

Heat oven to 450°. Squeeze soft garlic into a small bowl and mash. Set aside. Carefully scrub potatoes under cold running water to remove dirt. Place potatoes in the oven for 50 minutes. Slice potatoes in half lengthwise and carefully scoop out pulp without breaking skins. Mash or press pulp through a vegetable ricer. In a medium bowl, combine pulp with garlic, chives, milk, melted butter and 1 tbs. of the Parmesan cheese. Mix well. Refill potato skins with stuffing.

Reduce oven to 400°. Place potatoes in an ovenproof dish and sprinkle with remaining Parmesan cheese. Bake for 10 minutes. Place under a hot broiler for 4 minutes, or until golden brown. Serve immediately.

GARLIC-ROASTED POTATOES

Servings: 4

You can prepare these irresistible potatoes for any occasion. I recommend using a medium-sized freezer bag for coating the potatoes with the seasonings.

1½ lb. new red-skinned
   potatoes
¼ cup olive oil
4 large cloves garlic, minced or
   pressed

½ tsp. dried basil
½ tsp. dried oregano
¼ tsp. freshly ground pepper

Heat oven to 425°. Wash potatoes under cold running water with a vegetable brush. Remove eyes, but do not peel. Cut into 1-inch cubes. In a medium-sized plastic bag, combine all ingredients. Shake until potatoes are evenly coated. Place potatoes in a single layer in an ovenproof baking dish. Bake for 50 minutes. Turn occasionally.

MASHED POTATOES WITH ROASTED GARLIC Servings: 6-8

An old-fashioned hand masher leaves potatoes slightly lumpy. If you prefer, process with an electric mixer until lump-free and fluffy.

1 bulb *Roasted Garlic,* page 26
2 lb. potatoes, about 6
½ cup milk
¼ cup butter
¼ tsp. freshly ground pepper
chopped fresh parsley, optional

Prepare roasted garlic. Peel potatoes and cut into quarters. Place potatoes in a deep pot of cold water. Water should just cover potatoes. Cover pot and bring to a boil. Reduce heat and simmer for 20 minutes, or until tender. Carefully drain potatoes. Heat potatoes in pot over low heat to dry, stirring or shaking continuously.

Mash potatoes with a strong masher. Slowly add milk and mash continuously. Squeeze roasted garlic from each clove and add to potatoes with butter and pepper. Mash thoroughly. Transfer to serving plates or a warm ceramic bowl. Garnish with chopped parsley. For best flavor, serve immediately.

SPAGHETTI WITH GARLIC-BASIL CREAM SAUCE

Servings: 2

The Ancient Greeks rightly referred to basil as the "royal herb."

6 oz. dried spaghetti
¼ cup butter
4 cloves garlic, minced or
  pressed
1 cup light cream

1 tbs. plus 1 tsp. minced fresh
  basil
⅛ tsp. dried thyme
⅛ tsp. freshly ground pepper
freshly grated Parmesan cheese

Cook spaghetti in a medium pot according to package instructions. Melt butter in a small deep skillet. Add garlic and sauté for 3 minutes over low heat. Pour in cream and add 1 tbs. basil, thyme and pepper. Stir thoroughly. Simmer over medium-low heat, covered but vented, for 7 to 9 minutes, or until thickened. Stir occasionally.

If sauce becomes too thick, add more cream to thin. Pour sauce over spaghetti and sprinkle with fresh basil. Serve immediately with Parmesan cheese.

PASTA WITH TOMATO AND GARLIC SAUCE

Servings: 4

Garlic provides a stimulating flavor to this classic pasta entrée.

2 tbs. olive oil
12 cloves garlic, minced or
    pressed
1 cup minced onion
1 can (28 oz.) tomato puree
3 tbs. minced fresh basil
1 tsp. minced fresh parsley

1/4 freshly ground pepper
1/8 tsp. sugar
1 large bay leaf
12 oz. dried fettuccine or
    linguine
freshly grated Parmesan or
    Romano cheese

Heat olive oil in a saucepan or deep skillet. Add garlic and onion; sauté over medium heat for 7 to 10 minutes, or until soft. Add tomato puree and stir in remaining ingredients, except cheese.

Simmer with lid vented over medium-low heat for 1 1/2 hours. Stir occasionally.

Cook pasta according to package instructions. Remove bay leaf from sauce. Pour sauce over pasta and serve sprinkled with cheese.

BOW TIE PASTA WITH ROASTED GARLIC AND EGGPLANT
Servings: 4

The fontina cheese melts from the heat of the cooked vegetables and pasta for a truly wonderful dish with an interesting roasted flavor.

1 bulb garlic, roasted (see page 50)
6 cups eggplant, peeled and cut into 1-inch cubes
$\frac{1}{2}$ cup balsamic vinegar
4 tbs. olive oil
$\frac{1}{4}$ tsp. dried oregano
$\frac{1}{2}$ tsp. freshly ground pepper
3 cups chopped tomatoes , about 3 medium tomatoes
1 pkg. (8 oz.) dried large bow tie pasta
$\frac{1}{2}$ cup shredded fontina cheese
2 tbs. chopped fresh parsley
$\frac{1}{4}$ cup freshly grated Parmesan cheese

Heat oven to 425°. Separate roasted garlic cloves, peel and set aside. In a medium bowl, combine eggplant, vinegar, 3 tbs. olive oil, oregano and pepper. Mix thoroughly and marinate in the refrigerator for 1 hour. Place eggplant with liquid in a baking pan and bake for 25 minutes. Stir every 5 to 6 minutes.

About 10 minutes before eggplant is completely cooked, heat 1 tbs. olive oil in a skillet. Add tomatoes and garlic. Sauté for 5 minutes.

At the same time, cook pasta according to package instructions. Drain and divide cooked pasta on 4 serving plates. Cover pasta with roasted eggplant. Sprinkle with fontina cheese. Cover cheese with equal portions of tomato-garlic mixture and top with parsley. Serve immediately sprinkled with Parmesan cheese.

PASTA AND GARLIC CHEESE SAUCE

Servings: 4

For variety, substitute another vegetable for broccoli.

4 cups broccoli florets and sliced
  stems, boiled 5 to 6 minutes
16 oz. dried rigatoni pasta
1 tbs. olive oil
2 tbs. butter
3 tbs. flour
1 cup milk
1 tbs. minced fresh garlic

1 tbs. minced onion
2 tsp. dried basil
1 tsp. dried thyme
$1/2$ tsp. freshly ground pepper
1 cup shredded fontina cheese
1 cup shredded mozzarella
grated Parmesan for topping

Set broccoli aside. Cook pasta in a large pot according to package instructions. Drain and return to pot. Toss pasta with olive oil and cooked broccoli. In a medium saucepan, melt butter over medium heat. Stir continuously, slowly adding flour and milk. Add garlic, onion, basil, thyme and pepper. Mix well. Add fontina and mozzarella, mixing continuously over low heat as sauce forms, about 1 to 2 minutes. Pour sauce over pasta mix and serve with Parmesan cheese.

PASTA WITH ROASTED GARLIC & GREEN PEPPERS

Servings: 4

For a colorful appearance, prepare this dish with spinach fettuccine. Serve with fresh Italian or French bread.

2 bulbs *Roasted Garlic,* page 50
2 tbs. olive oil
1 large green or red bell pepper, diced
1 onion, minced
1 tsp. dried basil
½ tsp. dried oregano
¼ tsp. freshly ground pepper
4 cups *Marinara Sauce*, page 54
12 oz. dried fettuccine
freshly grated Parmesan cheese

Squeeze soft garlic from each roasted garlic clove and set aside. Heat olive oil in a skillet and sauté bell pepper for 3 minutes. Add onion and continue to sauté for 5 more minutes. Add pepper, onion, garlic and spices to *Marinara Sauce* and simmer for 30 minutes. Stir occasionally.

Cook pasta in a large pot of boiling water according to package instructions. Drain well. Distribute cooked pasta on warm serving plates. Top with a layer of sauce. Pass Parmesan cheese.

FETTUCCINE WITH GARLIC OIL

Serve as a main course or side dish with veal, poultry or seafood. For the best flavor, purchase Parmesan or Romano cheese in a large piece and grate it easily at home with a food processor or with a stainless steel hand crank-style grater.

$^2/_3$ cup olive oil
10 cloves garlic
12 oz. dried fettuccine

$^1/_3$ cup chopped fresh parsley
freshly grated Parmesan or
    Romano cheese

In a small saucepan, heat olive oil over medium heat. Add whole garlic cloves, reduce heat to low, cover and simmer for 25 minutes. Strain garlic and save oil. Set garlic aside to cool.

Cook pasta in a large pot according to package instructions. While pasta is cooking, squeeze pulp from garlic cloves and mash. Drain pasta and return to pot. Toss pasta with oil, garlic and parsley. Top with Parmesan or Romano cheese.

PASTA WITH ROASTED GARLIC AND BASIL SAUCE Servings: 4

Serve with a salad and garlic bread. The highly aromatic sauce is also delicious over freshly cooked vegetables.

10 cloves garlic	¼ cup chopped walnuts
¼ cup plus ¼ tsp. vegetable oil	3 tbs. chicken broth
1 tbs. balsamic vinegar	½ tsp. freshly ground pepper
1 cup chopped fresh basil	2 tbs. freshly grated Parmesan
¼ cup chopped fresh parsley	12 oz. dried linguine

Heat oven to 350°. Place garlic cloves in a garlic baker or on a nonstick or lightly oiled baking sheet. Cover and bake for 30 to 35 minutes. Peel skin from garlic cloves, or squeeze out garlic pulp.

Combine garlic, ¼ cup of the oil, vinegar, basil, parsley, nuts, chicken broth and pepper in a food processor or blender and process until smooth. Transfer to a bowl and stir in cheese; set aside. Cook pasta according to package instructions. Rinse and drain. In a saucepan, over low heat, toss with garlic-basil mixture and serve.

BAKED STUFFED SHRIMP

Roasted garlic and shrimp combine perfectly for dinner.

1 bulb *Roasted Garlic,* page 26
3 tbs. butter
¼ cup finely chopped bell pepper
1 small onion, finely chopped
½ cup breadcrumbs
¼ tsp. dried thyme

¼ tsp. freshly ground pepper
¼ tsp. salt
2 tbs. freshly grated Parmesan
8 jumbo shrimp, peeled and
  deveined
3 tbs. butter, melted

Heat oven to 400°. Separate roasted garlic cloves, peel and mash in a small bowl to form a paste. Melt butter in a skillet over medium heat. Add bell pepper and onion and sauté for 4 minutes. Add garlic paste and sauté for 3 minutes. Add breadcrumbs, thyme, pepper and salt and sauté for 3 minutes. Add Parmesan. Mix well and allow to cool. Butterfly shrimp and place in an ovenproof baking dish. Roll stuffing into eight 1¼-inch balls. Place a ball of stuffing on top of each shrimp. Drizzle with melted butter. Bake for 7 to 10 minutes, or until shrimp are pink.

SHRIMP AND GARLIC STIR-FRY

Servings: 4

This meal is full of flavor and colors. Most of the preparation can be done in advance. Serve over pasta or fresh lettuce for a variation.

2 tbs. peanut or vegetable oil
2 tbs. butter
2 stalks celery, cut into slices
1/2 cup sliced scallions
6 cloves garlic, minced or pressed
2 cloves garlic, thinly sliced
1 bell pepper, cut into thin strips

1 zucchini, cut into thin strips
1/2 cup dried sun-dried tomato pieces
1 lb. large shrimp, peeled and deveined
steamed white rice
1/4 cup almond slices, toasted

Heat oil and butter in a large skillet or wok over medium heat. Add celery, scallions and all of the garlic. Sauté for 3 minutes. Add pepper, zucchini and sun-dried tomatoes and mix.

Cover and simmer over low heat for 5 minutes. Add shrimp. Stir and sauté over medium-high heat until shrimp turn pink, about 2 to 3 minutes. Serve over rice. Scatter toasted almond slices on top.

SHRIMP SCAMPI

Absolutely delightful! This dish has 70 percent less fat than most scampi recipes and is just as flavorful.

1 medium bulb garlic, roasted for 45 minutes (see page 50)
1 lb. fresh or frozen large shrimp
2 tbs. butter
4 cloves garlic, minced or pressed
2 tbs. olive oil
1/3 cup dry sherry
2 tbs. fresh lemon juice
1 tbs. chopped fresh parsley
1/4 tsp. salt, optional
6 oz. spinach fettuccine, cooked according to package
   instructions, optional

Heat oven to 450°. Squeeze roasted garlic into a small bowl and set aside. Peel and devein shrimp. Wash under cold running water and pat dry.

Melt butter in a small saucepan. Add minced garlic, olive oil, sherry, lemon juice, parsley and salt. Place shrimp in a shallow ovenproof baking dish. Do not allow shrimp to overlap. Arrange roasted garlic cloves among shrimp.

Pour sauce over shrimp and garlic cloves. Bake for 5 minutes. Place under a preheated broiler for 5 minutes.

Serve immediately on warm individual serving plates or over hot spinach fettuccine.

PAN-FRIED SWORDFISH WITH GARLIC SALSA

Servings: 2

This is simple to prepare, spicy and satisfying. The salsa gives this dish a vibrant presentation. For an alternative, substitute fresh sea bass, tuna or bluefish.

2 swordfish steaks, 8 oz. each
1 tbs. olive oil
1/4 tsp. freshly ground pepper
1/2 cup *Garlic Salsa*, page 17
fresh parsley sprigs for garnish

Rinse fish under cold running water and pat dry. Heat olive oil over medium heat in a nonstick skillet and add pepper. Place fish in skillet and cook for 4 minutes. Turn fish over and spread a layer of *Garlic Salsa* on cooked side. Cover skillet and cook on medium-low heat for 4 more minutes. Transfer fish to serving plates. Serve with remaining salsa on the side for dipping. Garnish with parsley sprigs.

SPICY TUNA STEAKS

A nonstick grilling rack designed for cooking on an outdoor barbecue is perfect for keeping delicate foods from sticking, burning and falling apart. These are delicious with roasted vegetables.

1/4 cup vegetable or olive oil
6 cloves garlic, minced or
   pressed
3 tbs. low-sodium soy sauce
1/4 tsp. dry mustard

3 tbs. fresh lemon juice
1/2 tsp. freshly ground pepper
2 lb. tuna steaks
1 lemon, cut into wedges

In a medium bowl, combine oil, garlic, soy sauce, mustard, lemon juice and pepper. Mix well. Rinse fish under cold running water and pat dry. Place fish in a shallow bowl and cover with marinade. Refrigerate for 1 hour. Cook fish under a preheated broiler for 5 to 7 minutes on each side, or until opaque, or grill fish on an outdoor barbecue. Pour sauce over fish and serve with lemon wedges.

BAKED COD

You can replace cod with halibut, red snapper, flounder or haddock. Find a good fish market where you're sure the fish is fresh.

4 cod steaks, 8 oz. each
2 tsp. dried lemon peel
1 cup breadcrumbs
1 cup skim milk
¼ tsp. vegetable or olive oil
2 tbs. fresh lemon juice

1 tsp. minced fresh tarragon, or
 ½ tsp. dried
2 cloves garlic, minced or
 pressed
2 tbs. *Garlic Herb Butter*, page 23

Heat oven to 400°. Rinse fish under cold running water and pat dry. In a shallow bowl, mix together lemon peel and breadcrumbs. Pour milk in another shallow bowl and coat all sides of fish with milk. Dredge fish with breadcrumbs and place in a lightly oiled ovenproof baking dish. Drizzle with lemon juice and sprinkle with tarragon and garlic. Dot with *Garlic Herb Butter*.

Bake for 8 to 10 minutes, or until fish is just opaque.

HALIBUT WITH SUN-DRIED TOMATO PESTO

Servings: 4

Refrigerate extra pesto and use it as a dip or with fresh pasta.

2 cloves garlic
$1/4$ cup chopped sun-dried
   tomatoes, reconstituted
$1/4$ cup chopped fresh tomatoes
1 cup fresh basil leaves
$1/2$ cup olive oil

$1/4$ cup pine nuts or walnuts
$1/8$ tsp. freshly ground pepper
$1/4$ cup grated Parmesan cheese
4 halibut steaks, 8 oz. each
$1/2$ tsp. butter, room temperature
fresh parsley or cilantro for garnish

Heat oven to 475°. Make pesto: combine garlic, sun-dried tomatoes, fresh tomatoes, basil, olive oil, nuts and pepper in a blender or food processor. Puree for 15 to 20 seconds, until a paste forms. Pour into a bowl and mix in Parmesan cheese. Set aside.

Rinse fish under cold running water and pat dry; place in 1 large or 4 individual lightly buttered dishes. Spread a layer of pesto over each piece of fish. Cover with aluminum foil or parchment paper. Bake for 20 minutes. Garnish with fresh parsley or cilantro sprigs.

BAKED SALMON WITH SLICED GARLIC

Servings: 4

My dad, an avid salt water fisherman and fabulous cook, once told me that the secret to great-tasting salmon is simple. Just be sure it's fresh and cook it with lots of garlic. Add a garden salad and fresh rolls. Absolutely perfect!

2 lb. salmon
1/3 cup olive oil
4 cloves garlic, cut into slices

1/4 tsp. dried basil
1/4 tsp. dried parsley
1/4 tsp. freshly ground pepper

Heat oven to 375°. Rinse fish under cold running water and pat dry. Cut fish into 4 equal pieces and place in a shallow stainless steel or ceramic baking dish. Liberally coat all sides of fish with some of the olive oil. Do not allow fish pieces to overlap. Pour remaining olive oil over fish. Cover top layers of fish with garlic slices. Sprinkle with basil, parsley and pepper. Bake uncovered for 20 minutes.

CHICKEN AND GARLIC STIR-FRY

Servings: 2

This dish is tasty, beautiful, economical, and low-fat. As with most Chinese dishes, prepare all ingredients before you begin to cook.

1 cup white rice
2 chicken breast halves, skinned and boned
2 tbs. safflower, sunflower or peanut oil
1/4 cup low sodium soy sauce
1/2 tsp. grated fresh ginger
4 large cloves garlic, sliced
3 medium carrots, peeled and cut into thin matchstick strips
4 cups broccoli florets and chopped stems
2 tbs. water

Prepare rice in a steamer or saucepan. Rinse chicken, pat dry and cut into 1-inch cubes. Heat oil over medium-high heat in a large skillet or wok. Add chicken and sauté for 4 to 5 minutes. Reduce heat to medium. Add soy sauce, ginger, garlic, carrots, broccoli and water. Stir, cover and reduce heat to a low simmer for 5 minutes. Remove from skillet and serve over rice.

CHICKEN WITH 30 CLOVES OF GARLIC

Servings: 4

Thirty cloves of garlic, slowly cooked, create a sauce with splendid aromas and a surprisingly subtle garlic flavor.

2½–3 lb. chicken pieces
2 tbs. butter
1¼ cups chicken broth
½ cup white wine
½ cup tomato juice
2 tbs. flour

30 cloves garlic
1 bay leaf
1 tsp. dried thyme
¼ tsp. freshly ground pepper
¼ tsp. salt
cooked white rice or pasta

Rinse chicken pieces and pat dry. Heat butter in a large skillet and brown chicken pieces on each side over medium-high heat. Remove chicken from skillet and set aside. Add chicken broth, wine, tomato juice and flour to skillet. Stir and bring to a boil. Reduce heat to low. Add garlic, bay leaf, thyme, pepper, salt and chicken. Cover and simmer for 75 minutes. Remove chicken. Pour sauce through a gravy separator, or skim off fat from top of liquid. Serve with rice or pasta and top with sauce.

SKEWERED CHICKEN WITH SLICED GARLIC

Servings: 4

I use a garlic "mandolin" for slicing the garlic thinly. It's easy to use and is available at most gourmet shops. Serve these kabobs with white rice and a garden salad.

4 chicken breast halves,
  skinned, boned, and rinsed
1 cup *Garlicky Vinaigrette*, page
  22

1 large green bell pepper
1 large white or red onion
16 cloves garlic
1 large tomato

Cut chicken into 1-inch cubes. Combine with vinaigrette in a large bowl and marinate in the refrigerator for 2 hours. Cut pepper into 1-inch pieces. Cut onion into quarters and separate layers. Peel and slice garlic thinly. Cut tomato into 8 wedges, then cut each in half to create 16 pieces. Alternately thread chicken cubes, garlic, pepper, garlic, onion, garlic and tomato pieces onto eight 10-inch metal or presoaked bamboo skewers. Thread slices of garlic between pieces of food. Place skewers in a preheated broiler or on a medium-high grill and cook for 10 to 12 minutes. Turn and brush with marinade occasionally.

CHICKEN GARLIC PESTO

Servings: 4

Serve as a robust lunch or dinner with fresh vegetables and garlic bread. Pesto is wonderful tossed with hot pasta, used as a topping for pizza, and for many other uses.

PESTO

2 cups fresh basil leaves
3 cloves garlic
1 cup olive oil

$\frac{1}{2}$ cup pine nuts or walnuts
$\frac{1}{2}$ tsp. freshly ground pepper
$\frac{1}{2}$ cup freshly grated Parmesan

Combine all ingredients in a food processor or blender container. Process for 15 to 20 seconds, or until a paste forms. Set aside.

1 whole chicken, 4-5 lb.
1 clove garlic, thinly sliced
1 tbs. olive oil
1/4 tsp. dried thyme

1/4 tsp. freshly ground pepper
2 tbs. butter, melted
fresh lettuce

Heat oven to 325°. Remove giblets from chicken. Rinse chicken and pat dry. Tuck garlic slices under skin and rub skin with olive oil. Sprinkle chicken with thyme and pepper. Place chicken on a rack, breast side up, in a shallow ovenproof roasting pan.

Bake for 2 to 2 1/2 hours, or until chicken temperature reaches 180° on an instant-read meat thermometer. Baste with butter and pan drippings every 15 to 20 minutes. Remove from oven and cool. Discard skin and cut meat into bite-sized pieces. Toss chicken pieces with pesto. Serve warm or cold on lettuce-lined serving plates.

JOANNE'S CHICKEN AND GARLIC CHILI

Servings: 4-6

My wife Joanne worked with me on developing this special collection of delicious garlic recipes. She is truly a gifted cook. This is her own version of chili. It's the best I've ever had!

1 tbs. olive oil
6 cloves garlic, minced or pressed
2 medium onions, diced
2 medium green bell peppers, diced
2 cans (14.5 oz. cans) stewed tomatoes, chopped, with juice

1 can (15.5 oz.) pinto beans, drained
1 can (28 oz.) crushed tomatoes
1 tsp. ground cumin
6 tbs. chili powder
1/3 cup all-purpose flour
1 lb. chicken, cooked and sliced

In a large stockpot, heat olive oil and sauté garlic, onions and green peppers over medium heat until tender. Add remaining ingredients and mix well. Bring to a boil, reduce heat to low, cover and simmer for 1 1/2 hours.

BAKED GARLIC AND HERB CHICKEN BREASTS   Servings: 4

This is an ideal mid-week recipe for someone with a busy schedule. Just prepare the dish before you go to work and place the chicken in the oven when you get home, allowing yourself plenty of time to put together a fresh garden salad.

4 chicken breast halves, skinned
  and boned
1/4 cup olive oil
3 tbs. fresh lemon juice
4 cloves garlic, minced or pressed

2 tbs. minced onion
1 tsp. dried basil
1 tsp. dried thyme
1/2 tsp. freshly ground pepper

Rinse chicken under cold water and pat dry. Combine all ingredients, except chicken, in a bowl and mix thoroughly. Arrange chicken breasts in an ovenproof baking dish in one layer and cover with garlic-herb marinade. Refrigerate for at least 2 hours, or overnight.

Heat oven to 375°. Bake chicken in marinade for 40 minutes.

CHICKEN CUTLETS

This recipe can easily be adapted, and can be prepared a day in advance. Just reheat in a 325° oven for 10 to 15 minutes.

4 chicken breast halves,
   skinned, boned and rinsed
1 cup seasoned breadcrumbs
½ tsp. garlic powder
2 tbs. freshly grated Parmesan

½ tsp. dried basil
¼ tsp. freshly ground pepper
½ cup olive oil
1 egg, beaten

Fillet each chicken breast into 3 thin cutlets. Tenderize each cutlet with a wooden or metal mallet. In a shallow bowl, combine breadcrumbs, garlic powder, cheese, basil and pepper.

Heat olive oil over medium heat in a large skillet. Start with 3 tbs. olive oil and add more as needed. If cooking in an electric frying pan, set temperature at 350°. Dip cutlets in egg and coat with breadcrumb mixture. Shake off excess. Sauté each piece of chicken for 5 to 6 minutes on each side, or until golden brown. Place cooked cutlets on a paper towel-lined platter to absorb excess oil.

BISTRO GARLIC CHICKEN

Stuffed chicken breasts are topped with tomato sauce and cheese.

6 cloves garlic, minced or pressed
1/3 cup minced sun-dried
   tomatoes, reconstituted
1/2 cup minced marinated
   artichoke hearts
1/4 cup minced black olives
1/4 cup minced bell pepper
2 tbs. minced onion

1/2 tsp. dried basil
1/4 tsp. freshly ground pepper
8 chicken breast halves,
   skinned, boned and rinsed
3 cups tomato sauce
1/2 cup shredded fontina cheese
1 tbs. grated Parmesan cheese
chopped fresh parsley for garnish

Heat oven to 375°. In a medium bowl, combine garlic, sun-dried tomatoes, artichoke hearts, olives, bell pepper, onion, basil and pepper. Mix thoroughly. Place 4 chicken breast halves in an ovenproof casserole. Spread 1/4 of mixture on top of each breast. Cover each breast with another chicken breast. Spoon tomato sauce on top of chicken and sprinkle with fontina and Parmesan cheeses. Bake uncovered for 40 minutes. Garnish with parsley and serve.

CHICKEN FAJITAS

An oval cast iron or anodized aluminum skillet is ideal for preparing fajitas. It heats up quickly and maintains the temperature.

4 chicken breast halves, skinned and boned
3 cloves garlic, pressed
3 tbs. olive oil
1/4 cup fresh lime juice
1/2 tsp. dried oregano
1/2 tsp. freshly ground pepper
8 corn or flour tortillas
shredded lettuce, refried beans, chopped onions, guacamole, salsa and sour cream, optional

Rinse chicken and pat dry. Cut chicken into long strips, about 1/2-inch wide. In a shallow bowl, combine garlic, 2 tbs. olive oil, lime juice, oregano and pepper. Mix well. Add chicken strips, cover and refrigerate for 2 hours or overnight. Turn occasionally in marinade.

Heat 1 tbs. olive oil in a preheated skillet. Add chicken and cook over medium-high heat for 1 minute on each side, or until browned and cooked. Serve with warm tortillas and desired fillings.

LEMON GARLIC CHICKEN

This robust dish is for the more adventuresome.

1 egg
2 tbs. milk
2 chicken breast halves,
    skinned, boned and rinsed
1/2 cup flour
1 tbs. olive oil
1 cup chicken broth

1/4 cup dry sherry
juice of 1/2 lemon
1 tbs. chopped garlic
2 tbs. chopped fresh basil
8 oz. dried bow tie pasta
1/4 tsp. freshly ground pepper
2 tbs. freshly grated Parmesan

Combine egg and milk in a shallow bowl. Dip chicken in egg-milk mixture. Coat with flour and shake off excess. Heat olive oil in a skillet and sauté chicken for 5 minutes on each side. Add chicken broth, sherry, lemon juice and garlic. Bring to a boil. Cover skillet, reduce heat and simmer for 20 minutes. Add basil during last 5 minutes of cooking. While chicken is cooking, cook pasta and drain. Place chicken on a serving plate with pasta and pour lemon-garlic sauce over. Sprinkle with pepper and Parmesan cheese.

LEMON GARLIC VEAL

The garlic is the key to this delicious sauce. Serve with linguine.

1 large egg
1/2 lb. veal cutlets
1/4 cup flour
1/8 tsp. freshly ground pepper
1/4 cup butter

2 tbs. olive oil
4 cloves garlic, thinly sliced
2 tbs. fresh lemon juice
1 tbs. minced fresh basil

Beat egg in a shallow bowl. Cut and pound veal into thin pieces. Dip veal in egg and dredge in flour. Season both sides of veal with pepper.

Melt 2 tbs. of the butter in a skillet. Sauté veal over medium heat on each side for 2 to 3 minutes, or until brown. While veal is cooking, heat 2 tbs. olive oil and remaining 2 tbs. butter in a small skillet. Add garlic, lemon juice and basil. Sauté over medium heat for 4 minutes. Place cooked veal on 2 individual warm serving plates. Cover each plate of veal with half the sauce and serve.

ROAST PORK WITH GARLIC SLICES

Servings: 4

To reduce the garlic odor from your breath, try eating 2 or 3 sprigs of flat-leaf (Italian) parsley after a meal. It doesn't totally eliminate the odor, but it helps.

1 pork loin, about 4–5 lb.,
  boned
5 cloves garlic, cut in half
1 tbs. olive oil
¼ tsp. dried thyme

¼ tsp. dried rosemary
¼ tsp. dried sage
¼ tsp. freshly ground pepper
1 medium onion, thinly sliced
8–10 small red-skinned
  potatoes, quartered

Heat oven to 350°. Cut garlic cloves in half. Make 10 random slits in roast. Insert a piece of garlic into each slit. Rub roast with olive oil and season with thyme, rosemary, sage and pepper. Place pork loin in a roasting pan; surround with onion slices and potatoes. Bake for 2 hours, or until pork reaches 160° on an instant-read meat thermometer. Remove meat and potatoes from roasting pan. Allow roast to rest for at least 10 minutes before carving.

GARLIC-FLAVORED PORK CHOPS

This basic dish is easy to prepare, flavorful and very succulent.

¼ cup skim milk
¼ cup seasoned breadcrumbs
¼ tsp. garlic powder
1 tbs. freshly grated Parmesan
  cheese

1 tbs. chopped fresh parsley
¼ tsp. dried basil
¼ tsp. freshly ground pepper
4 pork chops, ½-inch thick
¼ cup olive oil

Pour milk into a shallow dish. In another shallow dish, combine breadcrumbs, garlic powder, Parmesan cheese, parsley, basil and pepper. Mix well. Dip chops into milk, coat with breadcrumb mixture and shake off excess. Heat olive oil in a skillet and sauté chops gently over medium heat for 5 to 6 minutes on each side, or until golden brown. Serve with mashed potatoes.

GARLIC-FLAVORED LAMB KABOBS

The distinctive flavors of garlic and lamb cook together beautifully. This makes an ideal informal summer meal. Serve with Hummus, *page 18,* Tabulleh, *page 42, and lots of small pita bread wedges.*

16 oz. *Garlicky Vinaigrette,*
    page 22
1 tsp. dried mint, or 1 tbs.
    minced fresh

2 lb. lean lamb
1 medium eggplant
2 medium red bell peppers
6 cloves garlic

Prepare a double recipe of *Garlicky Vinaigrette*. Combine with mint and mix well. Cut lamb into 1-inch cubes and place in a shallow bowl with marinade. Cover and refrigerate for 2 hours or overnight.

Peel eggplant and cut into 1-inch cubes. Cut peppers into 1-inch pieces. Peel garlic cloves and slice thinly. Alternately thread lamb, garlic, eggplant and peppers onto presoaked bamboo skewers. Place on a medium-hot grill or under a broiler for 15 minutes. Baste with marinade and turn frequently. Serve with rice and a salad.

BEEF AND GARLIC STIR-FRY

Servings: 4

Quick, easy and delicious. A delightful blend of vegetables and beef creates this exciting Chinese-style dish. Serve over white rice.

2 tsp. cornstarch
3 tbs. low-sodium soy sauce
1/4 cup water
1/2 tsp. sugar
1/2 tsp. freshly ground pepper
3 tbs. canola or peanut oil

5 cloves garlic, minced or
   pressed
1 lb. flank steak, thinly sliced
2 red bell peppers, sliced into
   matchstick strips
2 cups thinly sliced celery

In a small bowl, combine cornstarch, soy sauce, water, sugar and pepper. Set aside. Heat 2 tbs. oil in a large skillet or wok over medium-high heat. Add garlic and sauté for 20 seconds. Add beef and sauté for 3 to 4 minutes. Remove beef and set aside. Heat remaining oil in skillet. Add bell peppers and celery. Stir-fry for 3 minutes. Pour in soy sauce mixture. Add beef and stir-fry all ingredients for 2 minutes.

GARLIC MEAT LOAF

A garlic lover's delight! Serve hot or cold. Slice leftover meat loaf for fabulous sandwiches.

2 lb. ground chuck
2 cups breadcrumbs
1 egg, beaten
½ cup milk
2 medium onions, minced
2 cloves garlic, minced or
  pressed
¼ cup minced celery

¼ cup minced red or green bell
  peppers
2 tsp. Worcestershire sauce
1 tsp. dry mustard
2 tsp. minced fresh parsley
½ tsp. freshly ground pepper
¼ tsp. dried oregano
8–9 cloves garlic, thinly sliced

Heat oven to 350°. In a large bowl, combine all ingredients except garlic slices. Using clean hands, mix thoroughly. Pat meat mixture evenly into a meat loaf pan. Completely cover top of meat loaf with a layer of garlic slices. Bake for 1 hour and 15 minutes.

SLOPPY GARLICKY BURGERS

Servings: 4-6

In 1979, the first garlic festival in Gilroy, California, attracted about 15,000 people. Recent attendance has reached over 130,000 and the crowd continues to grow each year.

¼ cup bulghur wheat
½ cup water
1 lb. ground chuck
1 medium onion, minced
4 cloves garlic, minced or
  pressed

½ cup ketchup
½ tsp. dried basil
½ tsp. freshly ground pepper
¼ tsp. chili powder
pita bread or buns

Soak bulghur wheat in water for 1 hour. Sauté meat and onions in a nonstick skillet until brown, about 5 to 6 minutes. Drain. Drain water from bulghur. Add bulghur, garlic, ketchup, basil, pepper and chili powder to meat. Mix thoroughly and cook over low heat for 5 minutes. Stir occasionally. Serve in sliced pita pockets or on buns.

BROILED STEAK WITH GARLIC SAUCE

Servings: 4

This garlic-flavored beef dish is really tender and has a wonderful flavor. It's also perfect for the backyard grill.

3 tbs. butter
2 cloves garlic, minced or pressed
1 tbs. olive or vegetable oil
1/2 tsp. dried oregano

1/2 tsp. ground dried rosemary
1/4 tsp. freshly ground pepper
1 T-bone or porterhouse steak, 1 inch thick, about 2 lb.

Melt butter in a small saucepan. Combine melted butter with garlic, oil, oregano, rosemary and pepper. Trim excess fat from steak. Preheat the broiler for 10 minutes. Place steak on a lightly greased broiler rack set 4 inches from heat. Broil steak on each side for 5 minutes. Spread layer of garlic sauce on top of steak. Return to broiler and cook until done. To test, insert an instant-read meat thermometer into center of steak. Thermometer should read 130° for rare, 140° for medium and 160° for well done. Remove steak from broiler and serve immediately on warm serving plates.

INDEX